Get out of your country...To a land that I will show you

Genesis 12 v 1

Abram's father, Terah, took his entire family to live in Haran, and Terah died there when he was very old. The Lord spoke to Abram and told him to leave Haran and go to another land, which God would lead him to.

They came to the land of Canaan

Genesis 12 v 5

God promised that he would make Abram's name great, and bless all of his people. Abram left Haran, taking his wife Sarai, and his nephew, Lot, with him. Abram was seventy-five when he left, and they entered the land of Canaan.

The woman was taken to Pharaoh's house

Genesis 12 v 15

They passed on to Shechem, and Abram built an altar to the Lord, who told him that his descendants would be given the land. There was a severe famine at that time so Abram travelled to Egypt. His wife was very beautiful and he was worried that Pharaoh might want to take her and kill him so they agreed to pretend that Sarai was his sister. In Egypt Sarai was taken to the home of Pharaoh.

They separated from each other
Genesis 13 v 11

Pharaoh treated Abram well because he thought he was Sarai's brother, but the Lord brought plagues upon his house because of her. He returned her to Abram and they left Egypt. Abram was very rich but as they all returned to the altar he had built to the Lord, they realised that the land could not support them all, so he and Lot went their separate ways.

He armed his 318 trained servants

Genesis 14 v 14

Abram stayed in Canaan and Lot went to Sodom, but the men there were wicked. God told Abram that his descendants – meaning all the people that loved the Lord – would be so many that they could never be counted. At that time there were many battles between kings, and Sodom fell. Lot was captured but when Abram heard about it he armed his servants and set out to rescue him.

Sarai took Hagar and gave her to Abram to be his wife

Genesis 16 v 3

Abram rescued Lot, and the kings he had helped blessed him. Abram then prayed to the Lord because he was worried about having no children. God promised him an heir, but told Abram that his descendants would be slaves for 400 years then he, the Lord, would judge their enemies. Sarai told Abram to take her servant Hagar as his wife and have a child with her, since Sarai thought she could not have children.

Abram named his son...Ishmael

Genesis 16 v 15

Hagar became pregnant with Abram's child and felt she was better than Sarai. This made Sarai angry and she treated Hagar so badly that the servant ran away. The Angel of the Lord told her to return and promised her that her son would be called Ishmael and would be great. She returned and Abram named his son as the Angel instructed.

He...looked, and three men were standing by him

Gen 18v2

The Lord changed Abram's name to Abraham, and Sarai's to Sarah, and promised to be the God of all Abraham's descendants. As a sign of this promise every baby boy and male slave was to be circumcised. He promised that Sarah would have a child but Abraham laughed because she was too old to have a baby. God said he would bless Ishmael, but would start the covenant with Sarah's baby. Abraham then circumcised every male in the camp with him. Later, Abraham saw three men outside his tent – the Lord and two angels.

Take your wife and two daughters, lest you be consumed in the punishment of the city

Genesis 19 v 15

Abraham looked after the three men. They told him that they were going to destroy the towns of Sodom and Gomorrah because the people there were so wicked. Abraham asked God to spare the cities if there were more than ten people living there who loved the Lord, and God promised. The two angels went to Sodom, and Lot looked after them and protected them from the wicked men of the city. The angels told Lot to take his family and leave before they destroyed the towns so that he would be saved.

Sarah conceived and bore Abraham a son in his old age

Genesis 21v2

Lot and his family escaped. They were warned not to look behind them but Lot's wife did and she was turned into a pillar of salt for disobeying God. Then Sodom and Gomorrah were destroyed by the Lord. Abraham travelled to Gerar, and said again that Sarah was his sister, and the king took her. God told the king she was Abraham's wife and he gave her back to her husband. Then Sarah had Abraham's baby.

God opened her eyes and she saw a well of water

Genesis 21 v 19

Abraham was one hundred years old when his son was born. He named him Isaac. Sarah saw Ishmael being rude about Isaac and told Abraham to send him and his mother away, which he did. Hagar cried to the Lord, afraid that Ishmael would die in the desert, and the Lord heard her and comforted her. He helped her see a well so that she and her son could drink.

Abraham went to the place of which God had told him

Genesis 22 v 3

God was with Ishmael and he grew up in the wilderness, becoming an archer, and getting married. One day God tested Abraham by telling him to sacrifice his son Isaac, to see if his faith was strong enough to do it.

God will provide for Himself the lamb for a burnt offering

Genesis 22 v 8

Although Abraham was very sad, he did not hesitate and they travelled to the place he had been told about. Abraham tied Isaac to the altar and was ready to kill him but God stopped him, knowing he was completely faithful. God provided a ram for the offering, and blessed Abraham.

An outline of the life of Abraham

In the land of Ur lived a man named Abram, with his wife, Sarai. One day while Abram was praying, God told him to gather all his goods and take his family out of Ur. God promised to lead him, and brought them into the land of Canaan. While they were there a famine occurred so they went to Egypt where there was food. Sarai was very beautiful and Abram was afraid Pharaoh might kill him because she was his wife, so he told her to say that she was his sister.

When Pharaoh saw Sarai he wanted her to be his wife, but plagues came upon him while she was in his palace. Pharaoh discovered Sarai was Abram's wife and sent her back to him.

It was easier to get food now so Abram took his possessions and journeyed to Bethel. Abram's nephew, Lot, also had plenty of cattle and they could not find enough pasture for them both and so they decided to separate. Lot went east because the land around Jordan looked good. He moved into the city of Sodom but while he was there a king made war with the city. After the battle many people were taken prisoner, including Lot. One man escaped and told Abram, so Abram gathered his servants and rescued Lot.

God had promised Abram a son but Sarai was now quite old. She had an Egyptian maid called Hagar, and decided that Abram should have a son with her. Hagar did have a son, and he was named Ishmael.

Abram spent much time in prayer and God told him that his name would be changed to Abraham, and Sarai's to Sarah. God assured him that Sarah would have a son.

Abraham was outside his tent one day when three men came to him. They were messengers of God and they told Abraham that the cities of Sodom and Gomorrah would be destroyed but they would warn Lot to leave. Sodom and Gomorrah were destroyed because of their wickedness, but Lot, his wife, and their two daughters were able to escape. God told them not to look back at the city but Lot's wife did and became a pillar of salt.

Sarah did eventually have a son and he was called Isaac. As Isaac and Ishmael grew up there were some difficulties between them and Abraham had to send Hagar and her son away. They left the camp with food and water, but this soon ran out and Ishmael became very weak. However, God promised to look after them and water was provided.

When Isaac was in his teens God spoke to Abraham. He was told to go up the Mount Moriah and sacrifice his son Isaac. Abraham was very sad, but still obeyed God. They built an altar, Abraham tied Isaac to it, but God stopped him from killing Isaac. Instead God provided a ram for the sacrifice.

Throughout his life Abraham trusted God completely and obeyed him always, and God made him the father of a great nation—the Jews.

Also in this series

THE STORY OF MOSES. The Israelites were slaves in Egypt and there were many of them. The king said that all the baby boys had to be killed but the midwives would not do this. Soon after, Moses was born and his mother made a basket of bulrushes, laid him in it and left it floating on the River Nile.

Find out more in Book 5